12 QUESTIONS ABOUT
"THE STAR-SPANGLED BANNER"

by Jamie Kallio

STORY
LIBRARY

www.12StoryLibrary.com

12-Story Library is an imprint of Peterson Publishing Company and Press Room Editions.

Produced for 12-Story Library by Red Line Editorial

Photographs ©: Everett Historical/Shutterstock Images, cover, 1, 15, 21; Joseph Sohm/Shutterstock Images, 4; EdStock/iStock, 5; Library of Congress, 6, 28; Robert Dodd/Library of Congress, 7; George Munger/Library of Congress, 8; EyeJoy/iStockphoto, 9; John Bower/Library of Congress, 10, 29; William Dressler/Library of Congress, 12; Harris & Ewing/Library of Congress, 13; Marina Riley/Shutterstock Images, 14; Aneese/Shutterstock Images, 16; Eric Broder Van Dyke/Shutterstock Images, 17; spaugh/iStockphoto, 18; Mark Stephenson/iStockphoto/Thinkstock, 19; Dennis Cook/AP Images, 20, 23; E. H. Pickering/Library of Congress, 22; lev radin/Shutterstock Images, 24; Al Messerschmidt/AP Images, 25; Fuse/Thinkstock, 26; Bettmann/Corbis, 27

Library of Congress Cataloging-in-Publication Data
Names: Kallio, Jamie, author.
Title: 12 questions about "The star-spangled banner" / by Jamie Kallio.
Other titles: Twelve questions about "The star-spangled banner"
Description: Mankato, MN : 12-Story Library, 2017. | Series: Examining
  primary sources | Includes bibliographical references and index.
Identifiers: LCCN 2016002345 (print) | LCCN 2016003086 (ebook) | ISBN
  9781632352880 (library bound : alk. paper) | ISBN 9781632353382 (pbk. :
  alk. paper) | ISBN 9781621434559 (hosted ebook)
Subjects: LCSH: Star-spangled banner (Song)--Juvenile literature. | National
  songs--United States--History and criticism--Juvenile literature. |
  Flags--United States--History--19th century--Juvenile literature.
Classification: LCC ML3561.S8 K35 2016 (print) | LCC ML3561.S8 (ebook) | DDC
  782.42/15990973--dc23
LC record available at http://lccn.loc.gov/2016002345

Printed in the United States of America
Mankato, MN
May, 2016

Access free, up-to-date content on this topic plus a full digital version of this book. Scan the QR code on page 31 or use your school's login at 12StoryLibrary.com.

Table of Contents

What Is "The Star-Spangled Banner"?

"The Star-Spangled Banner" is the national anthem of the United States. In 1814, a lawyer named Francis Scott Key wrote a poem called "The Defence of Fort McHenry." The words were later set to music. The song was called "The Star-Spangled Banner." Key was inspired when the United States defeated the British navy in the Battle of Fort McHenry. The battle happened during the War of 1812. Key was on a boat when he saw the US flag flying above Fort McHenry. When Key saw the flag, he knew that the US troops had held off the British attack.

A replica of the 1814 US flag flies over Fort McHenry in Baltimore, Maryland.

When Key wrote his poem, it came from a place of emotion and relief. He felt proud of his country. "The Star-Spangled Banner" became well-known as a patriotic song. It has special importance for the US military. The song is often played at the raising and lowering of the US flag. Usually, the anthem is also played before sporting events.

Vice President Joe Biden (left) and President Barack Obama sing "The Star-Spangled Banner" at their 2009 inauguration ceremony.

Many Americans follow a certain etiquette when they hear "The Star-Spangled Banner." People stand and face the direction of the flag. They put their right hands over their hearts. They also remove their hats. Many people sing along when the song is playing.

GO TO THE SOURCE

To read the full text of "The Star-Spangled Banner," go to **www.12StoryLibrary.com/primary**.

117

Years between the writing of "The Star-Spangled Banner" and when it was adopted as the national anthem of the United States.

- Key wrote "The Star-Spangled Banner" in 1814.
- Key wrote the song after witnessing the Battle of Fort McHenry.
- He was inspired to write the song after he saw the US flag flying over the fort after the battle.
- Today, "The Star-Spangled Banner" is sung before sporting events and military ceremonies.

Who Was Francis Scott Key?

Francis Scott Key was born in Maryland in 1779. His family was wealthy. The name of his family's farm was Terra Rubra, which means "red clay." His father, John Ross Key, fought in the American Revolution.

Francis Scott Key went to St. John's College in Annapolis, Maryland.

When he graduated, he studied law under a judge. In 1803, he moved to Georgetown. Georgetown was located only a few miles from Washington, DC. There, he enjoyed a successful law practice and wrote poetry as a hobby. He was also a religious man. He wrote a hymn called "Lord, with Glowing Heart I'd Praise Thee" that was popular at the time.

11
Number of children Francis Scott Key had with his wife, Mary.

- Francis Scott Key was born into wealth in 1779.
- He studied at St. John's College in Annapolis and went on to become a lawyer.
- He wrote poetry and hymns as a hobby.
- He did not support war, but he changed his mind after Great Britain invaded the United States.

Francis Scott Key

The War of 1812 featured many open-sea battles between US and British ships.

Key did not like the idea of war. But in 1812, the United States went to war with Great Britain. The British invaded several areas of the United States. The future of the new country was in peril. Key soon changed his mind about war. He wanted to help protect his country. He enlisted in the militia in Washington, DC.

A COMPLICATED MAN

Though Francis Scott Key owned slaves, he opposed slave trafficking. He even offered his legal services to a group of enslaved people who were fighting for their freedom. They had been illegally brought as slaves into Maryland, where slavery was not allowed. During one case, he represented an enslaved person who was accused of murdering his owner. When a mob came to the jail to attack the accused, Key guarded the door and would not let the mob in.

What Was Happening When the Song Was Written?

The War of 1812 is sometimes called "The Second War of Independence." The United States had earned its freedom from Great Britain during the American Revolution. The war started in 1775 and ended in 1783. At the time, Great Britain was a world power.

In 1812, Great Britain was at war with France. British warships also attacked US ships at sea. They forced US sailors to join the British navy. They also stopped US ships carrying goods to France. The British wanted sea merchants to pay trade fees before they would be allowed to pass.

The conflict between Great Britain and the United States got worse. The US Navy was not strong. It only had 16 warships. Congress also did not have enough money to fund a war. Wealthy businessmen had to lend money to Congress.

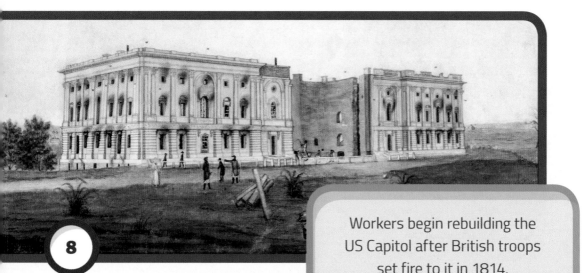

Workers begin rebuilding the US Capitol after British troops set fire to it in 1814.

Fort McHenry is strategically located on the Atlantic coast in Baltimore, Maryland.

The Americans tried to fight Britain in Canada, but their efforts were defeated.

In August 1814, the British raided Washington, DC. They burned the White House and the Capitol building. They seized weapons and military supplies. They went back to their ships and sailed toward Baltimore, Maryland. Fort McHenry was located in Baltimore. The US militia gathered there to prepare for an attack. The battle that followed inspired Key to write the poem that made him famous.

4,500
Number of British soldiers that landed in Benedict, Maryland, before their raid on Washington, DC.

- The War of 1812 is sometimes called "The Second War of Independence."
- Great Britain was a major world power.
- It was at war with France and restricted US trade.
- In August 1814, the British raided Washington, DC and burned several government buildings.

THINK ABOUT IT

Some people think "The Star-Spangled Banner" should only be sung at military and government events. They don't want it sung before sporting events. Others believe the song honors US values of pride and freedom. What do you think? Use this and previous chapters to support your answer.

4

Why Was "The Star-Spangled Banner" Written?

British troops planned a three-day attack against Fort McHenry in Baltimore. During this time, Key visited the British fleet. Because of his experience as a lawyer, he was chosen to negotiate the release of an American named Dr. William Beanes. British troops had taken the doctor prisoner. Key arrived at the British fleet on a ship flying a flag of truce. That told the British that the ship would not fire at them.

The British agreed to release the doctor. But they would not let Key or Dr. Beanes leave until after the attack on Fort McHenry. The truce ship was towed behind a British warship.

Early on September 13, the British began their attack. A thunderstorm struck at the same time. The British stopped shooting around dawn on September 14. Clouds and mist blocked Key's view. He used a spyglass to see Fort McHenry.

A print shows the bombardment of Fort McHenry by the British fleet.

STARS AND STRIPES

The stars that Key wrote about in "The Star-Spangled Banner" come from the stars at the upper-left corner of the US flag. The flag Key saw had 15 white stars, one for each state at the time. There were also 15 stripes: eight red and seven white. This number represented the original 13 colonies in the United States plus the two states that had since joined the country. In 1818 Congress passed the Flag Act, which returned the number of stripes to 13. But now, there are 50 stars: one to represent each state in the country.

1,800
Approximate number of British shells that blasted Fort McHenry in the attack.

- Key visited the British fleet to request the release of a prisoner, Dr. Beanes.
- Beanes was released, but neither he nor Key could leave until after the British attack.
- In the morning, Key saw the US flag through his spyglass.
- On his way to shore, Key wrote the first lines of what would eventually become "The Star-Spangled Banner."

He saw the large US flag flying over the fort. This meant the Americans had survived the battle.

Key and Dr. Beanes were free to go. As they made their way back to shore, Key took a letter from his pocket. On the back of it, he wrote the first few lines of his poem:

"O say can you see, by the dawn's early light,

What so proudly we hail'd at the twilight's last gleaming,

Whose broad stripes and bright stars, through the perilous fight

O'er the ramparts we watch'd, were so gallantly streaming?"

What Happened after the Song Was Published?

On September 16, 1814, Key finished writing about his experience. He originally entitled it "The Defence of Fort McHenry." The next day, Key showed what he had written to his brother-in-law. His brother-in-law submitted the song to a printer. The printer made posters and distributed them all over Baltimore.

The *Baltimore Patriot* and the *Evening Advertiser* were local newspapers. They published "The Defence of Fort McHenry" on September 20. Articles in the newspapers instructed that the words be sung to the tune of "To Anacreon in Heaven." This was a popular English song written in 1775. The tune was already well known.

Thomas Carr's music store in Baltimore soon published the words and music together. At this time, the song became known as "The Star-Spangled Banner." Newspapers around the country picked up the song. Soon, it became

Sheet music for the new song was published within weeks of the attack on Fort McHenry.

A copy of the lyrics in Key's handwriting

4

Number of verses in "The Star-Spangled Banner."

- Key finished writing "The Defence of Fort McHenry" on September 16, 1814.
- A Baltimore printer made copies of the song and distributed them.
- More newspapers picked up the song, and Carr's music store printed it with music.
- The first time the song was performed in public was October 19, 1814.

well known throughout the United States.

The first time "The Star-Spangled Banner" was performed in public was on October 19, 1814, at the Holliday Street Theater.

What Makes "The Star-Spangled Banner" Inspirational?

When the war ended in 1815, a feeling of nationalism grew in the United States. The young country came together in spirit and loyalty. The White House and Capitol building were rebuilt. As the population grew, Americans looked toward expanding west. The country was optimistic about its future.

Key reflected that pride and optimism in "The Star-Spangled Banner." The song captures an important moment in US history. His use of vivid imagery creates strong emotions in the listener. Lines such as "the rockets' red glare, the bombs bursting in air" reflect the harrowing battle Americans fought to keep their freedom. The words Key wrote continue to inspire Americans today.

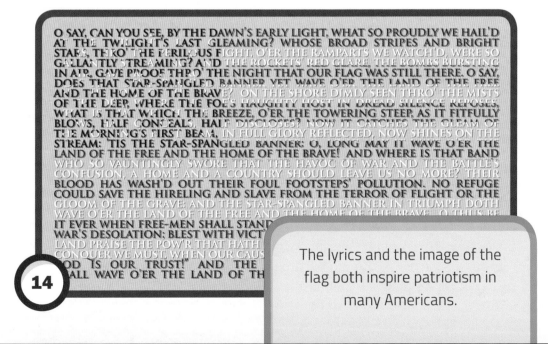

O SAY, CAN YOU SEE, BY THE DAWN'S EARLY LIGHT, WHAT SO PROUDLY WE HAIL'D AT THE TWILIGHT'S LAST GLEAMING? WHOSE BROAD STRIPES AND BRIGHT STARS, THRO' THE PERILOUS FIGHT, O'ER THE RAMPARTS WE WATCH'D, WERE SO GALLANTLY STREAMING? AND THE ROCKETS' RED GLARE, THE BOMBS BURSTING IN AIR, GAVE PROOF THRO' THE NIGHT THAT OUR FLAG WAS STILL THERE. O SAY, DOES THAT STAR-SPANGLED BANNER YET WAVE O'ER THE LAND OF THE FREE AND THE HOME OF THE BRAVE? ON THE SHORE DIMLY SEEN THRO' THE MISTS OF THE DEEP, WHERE THE FOE'S HAUGHTY HOST IN DREAD SILENCE REPOSES, WHAT IS THAT WHICH THE BREEZE, O'ER THE TOWERING STEEP, AS IT FITFULLY BLOWS, HALF CONCEALS, HALF DISCLOSES? NOW IT CATCHES THE GLEAM OF THE MORNING'S FIRST BEAM, IN FULL GLORY REFLECTED, NOW SHINES ON THE STREAM: 'TIS THE STAR-SPANGLED BANNER: O, LONG MAY IT WAVE O'ER THE LAND OF THE FREE AND THE HOME OF THE BRAVE! AND WHERE IS THAT BAND WHO SO VAUNTINGLY SWORE THAT THE HAVOC OF WAR AND THE BATTLE'S CONFUSION, A HOME AND A COUNTRY SHOULD LEAVE US NO MORE? THEIR BLOOD HAS WASH'D OUT THEIR FOUL FOOTSTEPS' POLLUTION. NO REFUGE COULD SAVE THE HIRELING AND SLAVE FROM THE TERROR OF FLIGHT OR THE GLOOM OF THE GRAVE: AND THE STAR-SPANGLED BANNER IN TRIUMPH DOTH WAVE O'ER THE LAND OF THE FREE AND THE HOME OF THE BRAVE. O THUS BE IT EVER WHEN FREE-MEN SHALL STAND ... WAR'S DESOLATION; BLEST WITH VICT ... LAND PRAISE THE POW'R THAT HATH ... CONQUER WE MUST, WHEN OUR CAUS ... OD IS OUR TRUST!" AND THE ... ALL WAVE O'ER THE LAND OF TH ...

The lyrics and the image of the flag both inspire patriotism in many Americans.

The flag and song served to boost the spirits of Union troops during the US Civil War.

"The Star-Spangled Banner" is part of the United States' identity. It is connected in symbolism to the US flag. In times of crisis, "The Star-Spangled Banner" helps to raise morale in many people. It can help reinforce pride in the country.

8 million

Number of people living in the United States in 1815.

- When the War of 1812 ended, the country was optimistic about the future.
- Key wrote "The Star-Spangled Banner" to express his pride.
- Imagery in the song helps inspire emotions in listeners.
- "The Star-Spangled Banner," like the US flag, is a patriotic symbol.

FIGHT SONG

During the US Civil War (1861–1865), the Union army sang "The Star-Spangled Banner." It became the unofficial anthem of the North during the war. The song became even more popular and revived patriotism in the US flag.

How Did the Song Become the US National Anthem?

During World War I (1914–1918), the United States still did not have an official national anthem. The US military used "The Star-Spangled Banner" as the unofficial anthem of the country.

The Veterans of Foreign Wars (VFW) and other patriotic groups campaigned to make "The Star-Spangled Banner" the national anthem. The song was competing with other patriotic tunes. "Yankee Doodle" and "America the Beautiful," among others, had support. Some people thought "The Star-Spangled Banner" was too difficult to sing. Others thought the words were old-fashioned.

Groups such as the VFW supported the push to make "The Star-Spangled Banner" the national anthem.

Still others thought a song about war shouldn't be sung during times of peace.

In spite of some opposition, Congress passed a bill making "The Star-Spangled Banner" the country's national anthem. On March 3, 1931, President Herbert Hoover signed the bill into law.

The national anthem is played before many sporting events.

1889
Year when it became common to stand while "The Star-Spangled Banner" was played.

- During World War I, the US military used "The Star-Spangled Banner" as the country's unofficial anthem.
- Some groups campaigned to make "The Star-Spangled Banner" the national anthem.
- Despite some resistance, "The Star-Spangled Banner" was chosen.
- On March 3, 1931, President Hoover signed the bill to make "The Star-Spangled Banner" the anthem.

THINK ABOUT IT

Symbols can mean different things to different people. What do you think of when you see the image of the Statue of Liberty?

How Is "The Star-Spangled Banner" a Symbol of Patriotism?

A national symbol represents a tradition, belief, or value of a country. Before Key wrote "The Star-Spangled Banner," the United States thought of the bald eagle as a national symbol. The US flag was just something to identify the country to others.

Key was inspired to write "The Star-Spangled Banner" when he saw the stars and stripes on the US flag fluttering over Fort McHenry. The flag and song are both strongly identified with the United States. The song is an expression of pride. The flag

The bald eagle was one of the first national symbols of the United States.

Many Americans have an emotional reaction when they hear "The Star-Spangled Banner." The song sparks a patriotic feeling for their country inside them. This is why "The Star-Spangled Banner" is often heard at emotional events, such as when the US military is returning home from overseas.

The US flag once had 15 stripes, but the Flag Act of 1818 made 13 stripes the standard going forward.

is a physical symbol of that pride. Together, they are both symbols of US values such as bravery and freedom. The language that Key used also symbolizes US values. He refers to the United States as "the land of the free and the home of the brave." Americans value freedom and bravery.

1787

Year the bald eagle became the US national emblem.

- A symbol represents a tradition, belief, or value of a country.
- Before "The Star-Spangled Banner," the United States did not have many national symbols.
- Many Americans feel a sense of patriotism when they hear "The Star-Spangled Banner."

THINK ABOUT IT

Use reference and online materials to learn about national symbols of the United States. How many can you find? What are some of them? What makes them US symbols?

19

9

How Has the Song Changed Since It First Appeared?

"The Star-Spangled Banner" has experienced some changes since it first appeared. For instance, the song has four verses. But today, rarely does one hear anything beyond the first verse. The original version was intended to be played and sung at a faster tempo than today's version. Usually, the song was performed by a soloist and not by a large group of people. Some historians claim that Key would not recognize it today.

After the song was first published in 1814, people sometimes changed the words to reflect the cultural issues of the time. For instance, when abolitionists were trying to end slavery, they changed the first lines to "Oh, say do you hear, at the dawn's early light/The

shrieks of those bondmen, whose blood is now streaming?" In 1861, US poet Oliver Wendell Holmes Sr. wrote a fifth verse to express his anguish over the US Civil War.

Sheet music for "To Anacreon in Heaven"

Sousa was known as "America's March King."

6

Number of verses in the song "To Anacreon in Heaven," on which the tune for "The Star-Spangled Banner" is based.

In later times, some musicians have changed the arrangement of the music in the "The Star-Spangled Banner." Russian composer Igor Stravinsky did this in 1941. His version was not well received by the public. An official arrangement of the song was composed in 1917 by US bandmaster John Philip Sousa.

- Today's version of "The Star-Spangled Banner" is slower than the original.
- Throughout the years, words were changed and additional verses added to reflect the changing cultural times.
- Several different arrangements of the song have been composed.
- Sousa composed the official arrangement in 1917.

Where Is the Flag That Inspired Key's Poem?

Mary Pickersgill and four teenage girls spent seven weeks making two flags for Fort McHenry. The smaller was a storm flag to be used in poor weather. The larger was a garrison flag, which was to be flown over the fort on special occasions. The garrison flag inspired Key to write his famous poem.

After the War of 1812, General George Armistead held on to the garrison flag as a family keepsake. Occasionally, he lent the flag to the city of Baltimore for special occasions. In the late 1800s, people began to request pieces of the flag as historic relics. This was a common practice at the time. The Armistead family gave away many "snippings" of the flag.

The house in Baltimore where Pickersgill made the Fort McHenry flags is now a museum.

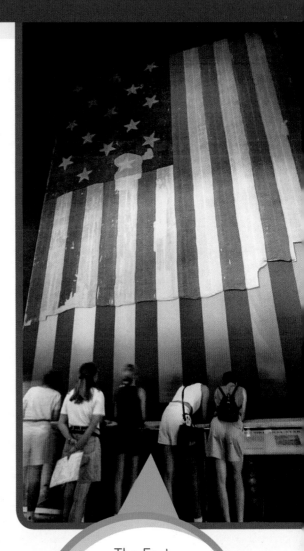

In 1912, the family gave the flag to the Smithsonian Institution as a gift. They directed the Smithsonian to always have the flag on display for the public to view. However, the flag was in poor condition when the Smithsonian received it. Conservators have been working to improve its condition for a long time. The flag is considered a national treasure.

$405.90

Amount of money Pickersgill received for sewing the two flags for Fort McHenry.

- Pickersgill and four teenage girls made two flags for Fort McHenry.
- One was a smaller storm flag, and the other was a much larger garrison flag.
- The garrison flag is the star-spangled banner that inspired Key.
- The Smithsonian Institution received the flag in 1912; it was in poor condition.

The Fort McHenry flag is now on display at the Smithsonian National Museum of American History in Washington, DC.

How Has the Song Appeared in Popular Culture?

For years, popular musicians have interpreted "The Star-Spangled Banner." Because the song is meaningful to many Americans, a good rendition of the song can make a singer very popular. At the same time, a bad rendition can make a singer extremely unpopular.

"The Star-Spangled Banner" can be difficult to sing. Often, a singer may not have the musical range needed to reach all the notes. It is easy to forget or mix up the words. If the singer is performing in front of a large audience, they may feel pressure to be perfect.

Many musicians feel honored to sing the national anthem. Some will try to add notes or other elements to make the song their own. Others will sing it in response to certain political and social conditions of the time.

> Singing the national anthem can be a stressful but rewarding experience.

750,000

Number of copies of Whitney Houston's version of "The Star-Spangled Banner" sold in the first eight days after its release.

- For years, musicians have interpreted "The Star-Spangled Banner" to make it their own.
- "The Star-Spangled Banner" can be difficult to sing.
- Many musicians have sung or played the anthem to reflect the political and social issues of the time.

Houston gave a memorable performance of the song at the Super Bowl in 1991.

In 1991, singer Whitney Houston opened the Super Bowl in Tampa, Florida, with a powerful rendition of "The Star-Spangled Banner." Her version was an enormous hit. It was rereleased 10 years later following the attacks on the World Trade Center. Most musicians agree that it is very hard to sing a perfect version of "The Star-Spangled Banner."

In 1969, guitarist Jimi Hendrix played the anthem at Woodstock, a rock music festival in upstate New York. This was during the Vietnam War. Hendrix mimicked the sounds of bombs and gunfire with his guitar.

What Does "The Star-Spangled Banner" Mean Today?

Today, "The Star-Spangled Banner" still has its critics. Many still believe the national anthem of the United States should be changed to something else. However, no one has made a serious attempt to challenge "The Star-Spangled Banner."

Many people in the United States regard the song as sacred.

Enthusiasm for the national anthem rekindled when the World Trade Center and the Pentagon were attacked on September 11, 2001. The attacks were considered some of the most devastating in US history. With its proud words and optimism, "The Star-Spangled Banner"

After 9/11, the country embraced patriotic symbols such as the flag, the Statue of Liberty, and the national anthem.

200,000

Estimated number of students and teachers who sang "The Star-Spangled Banner" simultaneously on September 11, 2015.

- Many people consider the song to be sacred.
- Enthusiasm for the national anthem was rekindled after the attacks of September 11, 2001.
- On September 11, 2015, students across the United States united to sing "The Star-Spangled Banner" at the same time.

The 1980 US men's hockey team celebrates at its Olympic medal ceremony.

gave many people hope that the United States would prevail.

That sense of patriotism has lasted. On September 11, 2015, students across the United States sang "The Star-Spangled Banner" at the same time. The national anthem is a reminder to Americans of the many battles the country has fought. "The Star-Spangled Banner" can unify the country in times of crisis and in peace.

OLYMPIC GOLD

Thanks to the efforts of some amazing athletes, "The Star-Spangled Banner" is given an international stage every two years. Whenever a member of Team USA wins an Olympic gold medal, the song is played at the medal presentation ceremony.

Fact Sheet

- The War of 1812 was mostly an offshoot of the Napoleonic Wars, which began in Europe in 1799 when Napoleon Bonaparte seized control of France. Bonaparte wanted control of the English Channel. He was defeated by Great Britain in April 1814.

- Shawnee leader Tecumseh joined forces with the British during the War of 1812. Tecumseh helped Great Britain seize control of Detroit in the United States.

- In August 1814, British soldiers raided the towns between Washington and Baltimore. Dr. William Beanes led a group of Americans to round up the disorderly soldiers. This incident led to Beanes's arrest by the British.

- Francis Scott Key's estate in Maryland, Terra Rubra, covered 2,800 acres. President George Washington once visited Key's family estate when Key was very young. Washington actually gave a speech from the front porch of Terra Rubra.

28

- The British surrounded Fort McHenry with 16 warships. Fort McHenry was built of brick and in the shape of a five-pointed star. The rockets Key describes in "The Star-Spangled Banner" were called Congreve rockets and did not cause much damage. After Fort McHenry survived the British attack in 1814, the US military band played "Yankee Doodle."

- The first time "The Star-Spangled Banner" was played at a World Series game was in 1918. The Chicago Cubs were playing the Boston Red Sox in Chicago. It was the first game of the series. During the seventh-inning stretch, the Cubs' band started to play the song. All the players and fans stood, took off their hats, and sang along. When the series moved to Boston, the song was played before the game. A tradition was born.

Glossary

abolitionist
A person in favor of stopping slavery.

anthem
An uplifting song of praise, usually identifying a particular place or group.

conservator
A person who repairs and cares for works of art or other precious items.

etiquette
Rules that explain how to behave in certain situations.

fleet
A group of warships under one commander.

imagery
Language that describes how someone or something looks, sounds, or feels.

militia
A group of people with some military training called to action during emergencies.

morale
The state of mind or spirits of a person or group of people.

nationalism
Loyalty and devotion to a nation.

patriotic
Expressing loyalty and support of one's country.

relic
An object treated with respect because of its connection to an event or person.

truce
A temporary halt to fighting.

For More Information

Books

Kulling, Monica. *Francis Scott Key's Star-Spangled Banner.* New York: Random House Children's Books, 2012.

Nelson, Maria. *The National Anthem.* New York: Gareth Stevens Publishing, 2015.

Wesolowski, Harriet. *The Songs We Sing: Honoring Our Country.* New York: PowerKids Press, 2013.

Visit 12StoryLibrary.com

Scan the code or use your school's login at **12StoryLibrary.com** for recent updates about this topic and a full digital version of this book. Enjoy free access to:

- Digital ebook
- Breaking news updates
- Live content feeds
- Videos, interactive maps, and graphics
- Additional web resources

Note to educators: Visit 12StoryLibrary.com/register to sign up for free premium website access. Enjoy live content plus a full digital version of every 12-Story Library book you own for every student at your school.

Index

About the Author

Jamie Kallio is a youth services librarian in the south suburbs of Chicago. She received a master of fine arts degree in writing for children and young adults from Hamline University in Minnesota and is the author of several nonfiction books for children.

READ MORE FROM 12-STORY LIBRARY

Every 12-Story Library book is available in many formats. For more information, visit 12StoryLibrary.com.